The Rise of The
Independents

Everything you need to write like a pro!

by

Nicole Mangum

Copyright ©2022 Nicole Mangum

All rights reserved. No part of this publication may be reproduced, distributed, or transmitted in any form or by any means, including photocopying, recording, or other electronic or mechanical methods, without the prior written permission of the publisher, except in the case of brief quotations embodied in critical reviews and certain other noncommercial uses permitted by copyright law.

ISBN: 978-1-951300-99-9

Liberation's Publishing – West Point - Mississippi

you're not here by accident
No not by far!
Love had you on His mind
before there were stars!

Table of Contents

Introduction 7

The Legalities 9

The Parts of a Book 13

What Makes Your Book Professional? 17

Unlock Your Creative Writer 23

Every Authors Secret Weapon 29

Let's Write a Book! 31

The Rise of the Independents

Introduction

The introduction of print on demand has given the independent author one of the greatest tools needed to become a successful published author. What is POD or Print on Demand? It is the option in the publishing world to print books as needed instead of printing bulk orders all at once. Before POD, publishing houses had to print all of the books they needed at once. This was very costly. With the invention of digital printing the world of book binding has become simpler.

POD has helped the indie author compete with the best. Gone are the days of indie author writing being considered subpar. Independent authors like LJ Ross author of *The DCI Ryan Mysteries Series,* USA Today Bestselling author Mark Dawson, and EL James *Fifty Shades of Grey* are just a few to be named. Let's not forget the trailblazers, Beatrix Potter and her independently published *The Tale of Peter Rabbit* nor Mark Twain and his *Adventures of Huckleberry Finn*. There are so many others, I do not have the time to make note of them all.

Deciding to become your own publisher and

branch out on your own is doable and can be successful. One only has to understand the industry and how it works. I have taken the time to break down the foundation of publishing, what makes a professionally published book, and how to distribute your book once you're done. Writing a book is such a rewarding career. I say career because once you write one book many more usually follow. At least for the serious writer. What I've set out to do is give you some powerful information to help you successfully complete your manuscript in a professional way. Once implemented your book will be able to stand beside any New York Times Bestseller!

As a published author you have many ways to earn money, aside from book sells. You can give talks, find new clients, consult, launch a product, become a coach, or build a personal brand. Of course, it's great to have a book that sells a million copies[1], but that's an extremely rare event even for bestselling authors. The more you see your book as a product and tool, the more successful you will become.

Let's get started!

---

[1] https://scribemedia.com/book-royalties/

The Legalities

The legal aspects of authoring a book are important. You may not think so at first, but you never know when your book will take off and become a bestselling work that agents are vying for. First thing first, Copyright. What is a copyright?

Copyright: the exclusive legal right, given to an originator or an assignee to print, publish, perform, film, or record literary, artistic, or musical material, and to authorize others to do the same[2].

Whenever you write anything, whenever you take it from your mind onto paper you have created a copywritten piece of work. Many confuse this inalienable right with registering "your" copyright. We will discuss registration in a moment. Once you write it and sign your name it is yours. Your thoughts are yours. In general, registration is voluntary. Copyright Protection is automatic. ***Copyright exists from the moment the work is***

---

[2] https://languages.oup.com/google-dictionary-en/

created. You will have to register, however, if you wish to bring a lawsuit for infringement of a U.S. work.[3]

Copyright Registration: The purpose of copyright registration is to place on record a verifiable account of the date and content of the work in question, so that in the event of a legal claim, or case of infringement or plagiarism, the copyright owner can produce a copy of the work from an official government source.[4]

Once you've finished writing your work you can electronically register it with the United States Library of Congress. It Usually takes 30 to 90 days to get your catalogue number. You will receive official papers in the mail. This paperwork will also allow you to transfer rights to your family or an organization after your passing.

ISBN: The International Standard Book Number is a numeric commercial book identifier which is intended to be unique. Publishers purchase ISBNs from an affiliate of the International ISBN Agency. An ISBN is assigned to each separate

---

[3] www.copyright.gov

[4] https://en.wikipedia.org/wiki/Copyright_registration

edition and variation of a publication. You can look at your ISBN as your book's social security number.

Bowker is the official ISBN Agency for publishers physically located in the United States and its territories (Puerto Rico, Guam, US Virgin Islands, Northern Mariana Islands, American Samoa, as well as military bases and embassies. If an ISBN is obtained from a source other than the official ISBN Agency, it might not identify the publisher of the title accurately. This can have implications for doing business in the publishing industry supply chain.[5]

Publishing Imprint: An imprint of a publisher is a trade name under which it publishes a work. A single publishing company may have multiple imprints, often using the different names as brands to market works to various demographic consumer segments.

Distributor: These are companies that pitch and sell books directly to wholesalers, bookstores, libraries, and other retailers through sale representatives and catalogs. There are three major distributors in the industry. Baker and Taylor,

---

[5] www.myidentifiers.com

Ingram, and American Family Warehouse.

Royalties: Royalty rates vary slightly, but on average, you can expect the following from traditional publishers:[6]

Hardcover sales: 15%

Trade paperback sales: 7.5%

Mass-market paperback sales: 5%

eBook sales: 25%

Audiobook sales: 25%

Independently publishing affords the author to keep an even greater percent of the profit. As one who self publishes you wouldn't get a royalty. You would receive the entire profit. This ranges according to the distributor you chose.

---

[6] https://scribemedia.com/book-royalties/

The Parts of a Book

A book like anything else tangible has to be put together. There are sections to your book, and they each have their proper place. Here they are!

Title Page

The title page is the first page you see when you open your book. It usually has the words formatted they same as the book cover.

Copyright Page

Here is where you place all of your professional credits. First and foremost, it's where you list yourself as the copyright holder. This page will also include ISBN, Library of Congress Number, Author reference, Illustrator, who ever took a part in the creation of the book. It is usually the first left-hand page after the title page, and it written in a smaller font.

Dedication

This should be centered on a right page. It can be written in a larger font than the rest of the book. It should be short and sweet, not confused with the acknowledgment.

Epigraph

This page usually places poem, a quote or lyric related to your book. (optional)

Table of Contents

Not needed for fiction writing, even though many have it. It lists Chapters and Subtitles.

List of Illustrations or Tables

Lists any illustrations, tables, that are placed in the book.

Foreword

This is a page for an introduction to your book that is written by someone other than the author.

Preface

This can list the books inspiration or notes on why the book is written.

Acknowledgements

Here is where you list all of the people, places or things that you'd like to acknowledge. This can also be located in the back of the book.

Prologue

The prologue is native to fiction writing and it sets the tone and scene for your book. It may explain somethings the reader needs to know to understand the story.

The Body of the Book

The Main Text

Here is all of the narrative of the book.

Epilogue

This is also native to fiction writing. It provides closure to the story.

Afterword

The preface for the end of your story.

Postscript

Additional information about the story. It can be used to create anticipation for the next book.

Back Matter

Appendix or addendum

This can contain references, background, list of important dates and time.

Endnotes

A table of the references throughout the book.

Glossary

A list of important definitions and or a list of your characters.

Bibliography

A list of all of your cited work.

List of Contributors

A list of names of authors. Usually used when multiple authors write a book.

Author Bio

This page which should be the last section is all about you the author.

What Makes Your Book Professional?

There are a few things that the publishing industry looks for in a professionally published book, but here is number one.

Proper Editing

Editing, as painstaking as it is, is the number one thing the industry looks for in professionalism. It is the stage when you and your editor do your due diligence to correct grammatical errors, to improve sentence structure, and provide a clear and concise manuscript. This can include adding sentences or words, deleting them, or simply rearranging them. Sometimes the correct placement of a thought changes the flow drastically.

This is primarily the most important part of your book. Editing is so much more than punctuation and grammar. Editing makes sure your story flows. Have you left loose ends? It keeps you from adding characters and never developing them. I've learned with many authors who write novels that they leave out dialogue through their writing. Instead of creating dialogue they may write. "Mary was so angry she felt like yelling." Create a dialogue, "I am so angry with you right now!" Mary yelled while spilling hot coffee onto her shirt.

Are you writing an adult book using grade school language? He said this. He did this. She was sad. This is a dead giveaway that your manuscript has not been professionally edited. Professionals in the industry can tell from page one if your book has seen an editor or not.

Freelance editors for hire can be found online or at your local University. Have your mind set to pay 3 to 4 cent per word.

Professional Cover Design

You cover is what makes a reader pick up the book in the first place. In a world where millions of books are released a day, your book must speak to the passerby. A professionally published book has a cover that suits its content, "brands" the book, entices readers, and is aimed squarely at the intended target market.[7] Covers should be readable

---

[7] www.thebookdesigner.com

and should give some idea of the content of the work. The font on the cover should be placed strategically. Not just plain on centered. The images on your cover can not be low pixeled phone selfie. Pricing should be listed on the back within the barcode. A publishing logo should be placed on the spine or back cover.

Your Font

I was had an author who insisted on publishing their book I all caps and use multiple exclamation points so that the reader could get the point. I tried and tried to explain that all caps make the eye tired, and the reader will put your book down never to pick it up again. Your font matters. The inside font should be clean lines that make the reader's eyes flow over the words. Your headers should be in place, the table of contents everything should be in place to make navigating your book easy on the eye and mind.

Genre Placement

You must consider where your book fits in the book market. Is it similar to other books already written? If so, how is your book better? Does it add more information? There has to be a niche that you want to conquer. Is it poetry, romance, religious?

Where does your book fit?

Marketing

How are you going to get your book noticed? I meet many authors who think that just because they have a good story the book will somehow magically sell itself. It will not no matter how great the story is. The world must be introduced to your new book. The best way to do this is to start developing a social media presence. I know it's hard to put yourself out there like that, but there is no other way. The public must know who you are and what you're doing. Google®, Facebook®, YouTube®, and Twitter® are suitable places to start.

There is no stream of income without marketing. This is true no matter the product. You book is your product. Resellers purchase it from your distributor with hopes of making a profit. You must look at your book this way and start talking and posting! There are authors who never sell a book through distribution. Look on Amazon® notice books that have never been ranked. They've never been sold.

ISBN and Identifiers

Your book needs its own ISBN number that points

it back to you. It also needs the proper metadata in place so that your book is easily found by any reseller.

Bookstore Returnability

Most book resellers will not consider housing your book without the guarantee of being able to return the book back to you if unsellable. When you contact a bookstore for an author signing or bookshelf space the two questions, they are likely to ask are, who's your publisher and it is returnable? You want to make sure your book distributor allows you to set this in place for your books.

Booksellers often buy independently published books on a trial basis to see how your book will sell in their store and test demand for your title.[8]

---

[8] https://www.ingramspark.com/blog/making-your-book-returnable

The Rise of the Independents

Unlock Your Creative Writer

Let's unlock the creative writer in you. We are focusing on fiction writing here. "Creative Writing" defined as writing that expresses ideas and thoughts in an imaginative way. The writer gets to express feelings and emotions instead of just presenting the facts.[9]

The Writing Process

1. What are you writing about? What do you want the reader to experience? Is this a mystery, a romance, a suspense, or a novel that should evoke some type of emotion?

2. Just write! Just start writing. This is not the time to try and put everything in sequence. You just want to write. From my experience as well as some of my author's, you're going to write multiple stories at once. Do not fret, you're going to go through this brainstorm and start to dissect each novel as well as

---

[9] https://grammar.yourdictionary.com/word-definitions/definition-of-creative- writing.html

multiple characters.

3. Outline your dissected pieces. Remember your outline is not written in stone. The story is still developing and it's okay to move around from one topic to another. Meaning, you may start developing the end of the story first, and that's okay.

4. Write the first draft, and do not worry about spelling and grammar so much. You're going to go through your story several times, and you will perfect it each round.

5. Share your story with other writers and readers. If someone doesn't read books, they may not be the best person to critique your book.

6. Take constructive criticism and rewrite the book using the input you've received.

7. Read and rewrite your work one last time checking for grammar and spelling. Send to a professional editor for last correction.

Character Development

1. Introduce your main character/s early in your writing. Make sure your reader knows their name and who they are to the story.

2. Describe your character, describe its mannerisms, how he/she sounds, his/her accent, is he/her attractive, plain, or ordinary. Your reader will paint their own picture of how they see your character based off of your descriptions.

3. Give your reader their background. Why are they the way they are or hint at it. Draw your reader in, make them love or hate them. Either way they will see him/her as a real person.

4. Make sure to share his/her weakness, you want your reader to identify with them either personally or relationship wise.

5. Draw upon your own experiences or those around you.

6. Do not bring in dummy characters and leave your reader wondering where they came from or where they're going.

Write Emotions

1. Describe what the emotion causes you to think or feel, is my best and easiest advice.

a. I loved him more than I should have.

b. I loved him with my every breath. It was as if

nothing else mattered. If he was sad, so was I. I spent money I didn't have to make sure he had everything to make him happy. I borrowed the money, stole the money, even sold myself for the money. It was all worth it to see him smile. But he never did.

Punctuations and Conversations

The most import thing to remember when writing is the keep the story flowing easily for the reader. It is not enough to say, "My wife nagged me to death." and leave the reader wondering, how? In what way? Words should flow and create a scene for the reader. Punctuation does this when done correctly. You want to indent for each new speaker.

1. Indent each time a new person speaks, let the speaker be easily identified, and use a variety of words instead of said or spoke.

"You promised you would help out more," Lisa yelled across the room.

John shot back, "I do help! I help more than you give me credit for."

"How! How are you helping, John?"

"I separated the clothes for you to do laundry."

"You see! That's the kind of crap I'm tired of."

John was furious, "And that's the kind of crap I'm tired of. You're always nagging, and I'm sick of it"

a. Quotation marks only around speech.

"I can't take another day of cooking for five people," said Hope as she looked at the pile of dishes her mom's company had left.

2. When identifying a speaker do not end the sentence between words. It is better demonstrated here

a. "It's cold out tonight," yawned Tom, "and I didn't bring another jacket."

These are just a few main parts to writing, and they give you a good head start. Understand most of all writing is not a weekend thing. It takes time, months sometimes even years to write a full rewarding manuscript. Don't be too hard on yourself. Ask for help. Read books to gain an ear for skillful writing. Take a class or sign up for a podcast. The world of publishing is no longer just available for those authors who are traditionally published. Sometimes traditions need to be broken.

The Rise of the Independents

Every Authors Secret Weapon

The reason I call the Chicago Manual of Style a publisher's secret weapon is because it has the answer to almost any question about editing, the correct wording, the correct way to cite another's work, accept or except and the likes of these things. It was published in t 1906 by the University of Chicago Press, on the largest and oldest University Presses in the United States.

It is the holy grail of professional writing. It is a jewel for the independent author. It can be accessed online or in print. Here is the website.

I recommend every serious writer to purchase this and use it to its full capacity. Very few independent writers know of this valuable tool.

"The Chicago Manual of Style is a style guide for American English published since 1906 by the University of Chicago Press. Its 17 editions have prescribed writing and citation styles widely used in publishing. It is "one of the most widely used and respected style guides in the United States".

The Chicago Manual of Style Online is the venerable, time-tested guide to style, usage, and grammar in an accessible online format. It is the indispensable reference for writers, editors, proofreaders, indexers, copywriters, designers, and publishers, informing the editorial canon with sound, definitive advice. Over 1.5 million copies sold![10]

---

[10] https://www.chicagomanualofstyle.org/home.html

Let's Write a Book!

After completing the steps outlines in this book you are now on your way to becoming a published author. Though this is not everything there is to know about the publishing industry I have given you the most important. This will get you into doors you probably felt would be closed forever. Now let's learn how to write a book!

Let's unlock the creative writer in you. We are focusing on fiction writing here. "Creative Writing" defined as writing that expresses ideas and thoughts in an imaginative way. The writer gets to express feelings and emotions instead of just presenting the facts.[11]

The Writing Process

1. What are you writing about? What do you want the reader to experience? Is this a mystery, a romance, a suspense, or a novel that should evoke

---

[11] https://grammar.yourdictionary.com/word-definitions/definition-of-creative- writing.html

some type of emotion?

2. Just write! Just start writing. This is not the time to try and put everything in sequence. You just want to write. From my experience as well as some of my author's, you're going to write multiple stories at once. Do not fret, you're going to go through this brainstorm and start to dissect each novel as well as multiple characters.

3. Outline your dissected pieces. Remember your outline is not written in stone. The story is still developing and it's okay to move around from one topic to another. Meaning, you may start developing the end of the story first, and that's okay.

4. Write the first draft, and do not worry about spelling and grammar so much. You're going to go through your story several times, and you will perfect it each round.

5. Share your story with other writers and readers. If someone doesn't read books, they may not be the best person to critique your book.

6. Take constructive criticism and rewrite the book using the input you've received.

7. Read and rewrite your work one last time checking for grammar and spelling. Send to a

professional editor for last correction.

Character Development

1. Introduce your main character/s early in your writing. Make sure your reader knows their name and who they are to the story.

2. Describe your character, describe its mannerisms, how he/she sounds, his/her accent, is he/her attractive, plain, or ordinary. Your reader will paint their own picture of how they see your character based off of your descriptions.

3. Give your reader their background. Why are they the way they are or hint at it. Draw your reader in, make them love or hate them. Either way they will see him/her as a real person.

4. Make sure to share his/her weakness, you want your reader to identify with them either personally or relationship wise.

5. Draw upon your own experiences or those around you.

6. Do not bring in dummy characters and leave your reader wondering where they came from or where they 're going.

Write Emotions

1. Describe what the emotion causes you to think or feel, is my best and easiest advice.

a. I loved him more than I should have.

b. I loved him with my every breath. It was as if nothing else mattered. If he was sad, so was I. I spent money I didn't have to make sure he had everything to make him happy. I borrowed the money, stole the money, even sold myself for the money. It was all worth it to see him smile. But he never did.

Punctuation and Conversations

The most import thing to remember when writing is the keep the story flowing easily for the reader. It is not enough to say, "My wife nagged me to death." and leave the reader wondering, how? In what way? Words should flow and create a scene for the reader. Punctuation does this when done correctly. You want to indent for each new speaker.

1. Indent each time a new person speaks, let the speaker be easily identified, and use a variety of words instead of said or spoke.

"You promised you would help out more," Lisa

yelled across the room.

John shot back, "I do help! I help more than you give me credit for."

"How! How are you helping, John?"

"I separated the clothes for you to do laundry." "You see! That's the kind of crap I'm tired of."

John was furious, "And that's the kind of crap I'm tired of. You're always nagging, and I'm sick of it"

   a.   Quotation marks only around speech.

"I can't take another day of cooking for five people," said Hope as she looked at the pile of dishes her mom's company had left.

2.   When identifying a speaker do not end the sentence between words. It is better demonstrated here,

   a.   *"It's cold out tonight," yawned Tom, "and I didn't bring another jacket."*

These are just a few main parts to writing, and they give you a good head start. Understand most of all writing is not a weekend thing. It takes time, months sometimes even years to write a full rewarding manuscript. Don't be too hard on yourself. Ask for help. Read books to gain an ear for skillful writing. Take a class or sign up for a podcast. The world of publishing is no longer just available for those authors who are traditionally published. Sometimes traditions need to be broken.

Welcome to the world Independent Author!

Nicole Mangum

The Rise of the Independents